Emergency Vehicles
Fire Truck

Chris Oxlade

QED Publishing

First published in the UK in 2009 by
QED Publishing
A Quarto Group company
226 City Road
London EC1V 2TT

www.qed-publishing.co.uk

A catalogue record for this book is available from the British Library.

ISBN 978 1 84835 266 7

Printed and bound in China

Author Chris Oxlade
Editor Eve Marleau
Designer Susi Martin

Publisher Steve Evans
Creative Director Zeta Davies
Managing Editor Amanda Askew

Picture credits
(t=top, b=bottom, l=left, r=right, c=centre, fc=front cover)
Alamy
5t Firephoto; 7r Blue shadows; 9r Blue shadows; 11 Jack Sullivan; 16r EuroStyle Graphics; 19r Michael Routh
Corbis
12–13 Patrick Bennett; 15 Transtock
Photolibrary
8–9 Charles Schuck
Pierce Manufacturing, Inc., an Oshkosh Corporation company
4–5; 6–7
Shutterstock
Tyler Olsen; 10b Christoffer Vika; 13t Monkey Business Images; 14 Mike Brake; 17–18 Christoffer Vika; 18–19 Ivan Cholakov; 20–21 Gaby Kooijman; 21r Slavko Sereda

Words in **bold** can be found in the glossary on page 23.

Contents

What is a fire truck? 4

Parts of a fire truck............................. 6

Pumps and hoses................................ 8

Fire truck equipment 10

Emergency! 12

Ladder trucks 14

Airport fire trucks.............................. 16

Cross-country trucks........................... 18

In air and on water 20

Activities 22

Glossary 23

Index.. 24

What is a fire truck?

A fire truck is an **emergency** vehicle. Fire trucks help **firefighters** to put out fires. They also help with other emergencies, such as rescues and floods.

In the United States, some cities use aerial trucks. They have a special long ladder.

Firefighters wear fireproof suits, helmets and strong boots to protect them from the heat of the flames.

Firefighters also pump away floodwater using the hoses.

Parts of a **fire truck**

There are many different types of fire truck.

Most trucks are called **pumpers** or tenders.

They are used in many different rescues.

Cab

This fire truck has a large water tank inside, a water **pump**, **hoses**, ladders and other special equipment.

Ladder

NORTH CANTON

Pierce

Ladders can be used to rescue people from windows in burning buildings.

Lockers

Pumps and hoses

Fire trucks have an on-board water pump. The fire truck's engine makes the pump work.

A pump can suck up 4000 litres of water into the hoses every minute – that's 30 bathtubs!

A fire truck carries lots of hoses. There are hoses to bring water to the truck's pump and hoses to carry water to the fire.

Firefighters get water from fire hydrants.

Fire truck equipment

Fire trucks carry lots of equipment that firefighters need to rescue people. There are metal cutters, **portable** water pumps, digging tools and **breathing masks**.

This firefighter is using a metal cutter.

The equipment is kept in lockers along the sides of the truck. Firefighters check this equipment every day to make sure it's safe to use.

Emergency!

Fire trucks and firefighters are always ready for action. When an emergency call comes, the firefighters jump straight into their trucks.

Flashing lights and noisy **sirens** on the fire truck warn people to move out of the way and let the truck through.

On top of an airport fire truck is a hose called a monitor. It sprays foam over a fire. The foam covers the flames and puts it out.

Cross-country trucks

Forest fires can be difficult to put out. The ground can be rough, and the fire spreads quickly. Firefighters use special trucks with on-board water tanks to fight forest fires.

This fire truck has a metal cage to protect its crew from falling branches.

Forest firefighters also use **four-wheel-drive** pick-up trucks. They carry water and equipment to put out small fires.

It can be easier to reach a forest fire in a four-wheel-drive truck.

In air and on water

Firefighters also work in the air and on the water. Firefighting boats spray water onto fires in buildings along river banks. They also help to fight fires on ships at sea.

Firefighting aircraft are often used to fight forest fires. Helicopters and **fixed-wing aircraft** drop water onto the flames from above.

Firefighting aircraft scoop up water from rivers or lakes and drop it onto the flames.

Port of Rotterdam

Activities

- Which picture shows an airport truck, a ladder truck and a firefighting plane?

- Make a drawing of your favourite fire truck. What sort of truck is it? Does it have lights and sirens? What colour is it?

- Write a story about a fire. It could be anywhere in the world – or even on another planet! What truck would you drive? How big would the fire be? How dangerous would it be? How long would it take to put it out?

- Which of these fire trucks would be used to put out a fire at sea?

Glossary

Breathing mask
A mask that lets a firefighter breathe in a smoke-filled building.

Emergency
A dangerous situation that must be dealt with straight away.

Firefighter
A person whose job it is to fight fires.

Fixed-wing aircraft
An aircraft with two-wings that are fixed to its body.

Foam
A frothy material made from water filled with soapy bubbles.

Four-wheel-drive vehicle
A vehicle with four wheels that are all turned by its engine.

Hose
A long tube that water flows along.

Portable
Something that can be carried around.

Pump
A machine that sucks and pushes water along hoses.

Pumper
A fire truck that is used in many emergency situations.

Siren
A machine that makes a loud noise.

Telescopic
When parts slide over each other to make something such as a ladder longer or shorter.

Index

aircraft 17, 21
airport fire trucks 16–17

boats 20
breathing masks 10, 23

digging tools 10

fire hydrants 9
fireproof suits 5, 13
flashing lights 13
foam 16, 17, 23
forest fires 18, 19, 21
four-wheel-drive vehicles
    19, 23

helicopters 21
hoses 7, 8, 9, 17, 23
hydraulics 14, 23

ladders 6, 7, 11, 14, 15, 23

metal cutters 10
monitors 17

pick-up trucks 19
pumpers 6, 9, 23

ships 20
sirens 13, 23

telescopic ladders 14, 23
tenders 6

water pumps 6, 7, 8, 9,
    10, 23
water tanks 6, 7, 9, 18